50 STATES TO CELEBRATE

Celebrating
CALIFORNIA

The text of this book is set in Weidemann.
The display type is set in Bernard Gothic.
The illustrations are drawn with pencil and colored digitally.
The maps are pen, ink, and watercolor.

Photograph of grizzly bear on page 32 © 2013 Photodisc/Getty Images
Photograph of California valley quail on page 32 © 2013 Photodisc/Getty Images
Photograph of golden poppy on page 32 © 2013 Photodisc/Getty Images

Library of Congress Cataloging-in-Publication Data:
Bauer, Marion Dane.
Celebrating California / by Marion Dane Bauer ; illustrated by C. B. Canga.
p. cm. — (Green light readers level 3) (50 states to celebrate)
ISBN 978-0-547-89697-7 (trade paper)
ISBN 978-0-547-98385-1 (paper over board)
1. California—Juvenile literature. I. Canga, C. B., ill. II. Title.
F861.3.B38 2013
979.4—dc23
2012016847

Manufactured in China
SCP 10 9 8 7 6 5 4 3 2 1
4500401385

50 STATES TO CELEBRATE

Celebrating
CALIFORNIA

Written by **Marion Dane Bauer**
Illustrated by **C. B. Canga**

sandpiper

Houghton Mifflin Harcourt
Boston   New York   2013

Hi! I'm Mr. Geo.
Welcome to the Golden State—California!
Here I am surrounded by golden sun
and golden sand.

Washington
Oregon
California
Nevada
Idaho
Montana
Wyoming
Utah
Colorado
Arizona
New Mexico
North Dakota
South Dakota
Nebraska
Kansas
Okla
Texas

PACIFIC OCEAN

C A N

M E X I C O

Alaska
*NOT TO SCALE

Hawaii
*NOT TO SCALE

California is easy to find on the map.
Go as far west as you can.
But stop before you get your feet
wet in the Pacific Ocean!

There's California!
It's north of Mexico.
South of Oregon.
West of Nevada and Arizona.

3

Lights! Camera! Action!
California is famous for making movies
and television shows.

I won tickets to see my favorite TV talent show.
The judges think that singer will be a big star!
I agree!

California is a lot more than
sunshine and show business.
It's a big state, a beautiful state, a state that
changes greatly as you travel from place to place.
I want to see it all.
California, here I come!

Let's start south at the San Diego Zoo.
Today, I am feeding the California sea lions.
One of them thanked me with a sloppy kiss!

San Diego is one of the oldest cities in California.
In 1769, Father Junipero Serra came from Spain
to start a **mission.**
Native Americans built the mission and did most of
the work.

Later, 20 more missions were built
along California's coast.
We can learn how people lived and worked
a long time ago at some of the missions.
I used my hands *and* feet to make these bricks!

Did you know?

Adobe bricks are made of dried clay and straw. They were used to build the 21 missions.

Next stop, Disneyland in Anaheim!

Want to rocket into the **galaxy** on Space Mountain?

Are you brave enough for the Haunted Mansion?

I'm not sure I am!

But I am sure I want to meet Mickey Mouse!

At Paramount Pictures in Hollywood,
we can see how movies are made.
That stuntman really knows his tricks!
Later, I'm going to a concert at the Hollywood Bowl.
I love listening to music under a starry sky!

Hollywood is a part of Los Angeles,
the second biggest city in the United States.
Most people call it L.A.
Los Angeles means "The Angels" in Spanish.
The only angels I saw were in baseball uniforms.
Go, Angels!

In the middle of this modern city, I found something very old.

It's the La Brea **Tar** Pits.

Mammoths! Saber-tooth cats! Giant sloths!

All were trapped in sticky tar long, long ago.

Wow! These bones were **preserved** perfectly!

Scientists are still discovering **fossils** of ancient animals and plants at the La Brea Tar Pits.

The Los Angeles area is great for outdoor fun.

Want to join me?

We can hike the Hollywood Hills.

Bike the path at Venice Beach.

Walk the pier in Santa Monica.

I like the view from up here best!

The Ferris wheel on the Santa Monica Pier is powered by solar energy.

15

California has high peaks and low lands.
Mount Whitney is the highest spot in California.
Death Valley in the Mojave Desert is the lowest.

Did you know?

The highest temperature ever recorded in
Death Valley is 136.4 degrees (Fahrenheit).
That makes it the hottest place in the world!

California is known for palm trees.

But the state's redwood forests are also famous.

Its coastal redwoods are the world's tallest trees.

The giant sequoias are the biggest.

Watch me drive through!

California is a fine place to live.

More people live here than in any other state.

But California has some **environmental** problems.

Smog sometimes fills the air.

Water shortages happen.

Earthquakes happen too.

Most are too small to feel, but some do great damage.

The strongest earthquake in California history took place in San Francisco in 1906.

When it is too dry, there can be wildfires.

When it is too wet . . . floods and landslides.

Still, about 37 million people call California home.

And new people move to California every year.

I love visiting here!

High or low, wet or dry,

California is full of wildlife.

Roadrunners and wild horses roam the deserts.

Lizards, too!

Hummingbirds flutter in flowery fields.

Raccoons and **opossums** scurry around the forests.

I saw jackrabbits in shrubs on the **chaparral.**
And did you see that rattlesnake slither by?
At the coast, seagulls and pelicans fly overhead.
Below, gray whales and seals swim the seas.

Early in its history, California was home to
thousands of grizzly bears. They have been
extinct in California since 1922.

Long, flat, and green.

A fertile valley lies beyond the coastal mountains.

Here, farmers grow fruits and vegetables aplenty.

Salad, anyone?

These tomatoes are fresh off the vine.

Do you like milk as much as I do?
Milk is California's leading farm product.
Grapes are next.
And nearly every almond and walnut you eat
comes from California.

Raisins come from grapes. They can be brown
or yellow . . . and chocolate-covered!

23

Let's not forget Silicon Valley.

It's a valley that grows computers.

Just kidding! Silicon Valley is a nickname

for a **region** in Northern California.

Many computer companies are located there.

Today, I'm at a museum learning how computers work.

They let me try on this "bunny" suit!

Workers use them to keep **computer chips** clean.

Cable cars.

The Golden Gate Bridge.

Crooked streets plunging to the bay.

Delicious seafood at Fisherman's Wharf.

Shopping at Union Square.

All of this is San Francisco!

The San Francisco streets are so hilly that every cable car needs three different **brake systems** for safety.

Chinatown is San Francisco too.

This grand gate welcomes all.

Thousands came from China in the late 1800s.

They helped build our nation's railroads.

They helped San Francisco grow.

So did people from many other **cultures**.

Gold also helped San Francisco grow.

It started in January of 1848.

James Marshall discovered gold at Sutter's Mill.

What followed was the gold rush.

People from all over rushed to the area.

They hoped to find gold and get rich.

Only a few found gold.

Many went home broke.

Some died.

Most ended up make a living another way.

Levi Strauss became successful making
blue jeans during the gold rush.

Eureka!

In Greek, *eureka* means "I have found it!"

It's what miners said when they found gold.

It's also the name of a city in Northern California.

And here I stand in Eureka,

looking over the Pacific Ocean.

Redwoods tower above me.
Mountains rise behind me.
I *have* found gold.
I've found the Golden State.
California!

Fast Facts About California

Nickname: The Golden State because of its golden sunshine, golden sand, and golden poppy flowers, and the gold rush.

State motto: Eureka . . . I have found it!

State capital: Sacramento

Other major cities: Los Angeles, San Diego, San Jose, San Francisco

Year of statehood: 1850

State animal: Grizzly bear

State bird: California valley quail

State flower: Golden poppy

State flag:

Population: More than 37 million, according to the 2010 census

Presidents from California: Richard M. Nixon, Ronald Reagan

Fun fact: A bristlecone pine tree called Methuselah is considered the oldest known living tree in the world. It is more than 4,600 years old and still growing in the White Mountains of eastern California.

Dates in California History

1542: Joao Rodrigues Cabrillo is first European to explore the area.

1769: Father Junipero Serra of Spain starts the first mission in San Diego.

1821: Mexico wins independence from Spain; California becomes part of Mexico.

1843: Americans begin traveling to California by the **Oregon Trail**.

1846–48: The Mexican-American War; California becomes part of the United States.

1848: Gold is discovered at Sutter's Mill.

1849: The California gold rush begins.

1850: California becomes the 31st state.

1869: The transcontinental railroad is completed, linking California to the rest of the country.

1906: A great earthquake, followed by fires, nearly destroys San Francisco.

1920s: California's economy booms due to fast growth in the movie, aircraft, and tourism industries.

1937: Golden Gate Bridge opens.

1955: Disneyland theme park opens.

1981: Ronald Reagan, a former actor and governor of California, becomes president of the United States.

1984: Los Angeles hosts the Summer Olympics.

2007: Wildfires burn more than 400,000 acres of land in Southern California.

Activities

1. **LOCATE** the two states on California's eastern border on the map on pages 2 and 3. Then, **SAY** each state's name out loud.

2. **IMAGINE** you are hosting a party someplace in California. Now **DESIGN** an invitation for the party. On the front of the invitation, draw a picture that represents the place. Inside, write why you chose that place. Give a time, date, and reason for the party too!

3. **SHARE** two facts you learned about California with a family member or friend.

4. **PRETEND** you are filming a movie about California. The people who work for you have lots of questions about the state. Answer the following questions for them correctly and your movie will be a big success!

   a. **WHO** started the first Spanish mission in California?

   b. **WHAT** types of animals were trapped in the La Brea Tar Pits long ago?

   c. **WHAT** desert is Death Valley in?

   d. **WHERE** is the Golden Gate Bridge?

   e. **WHEN** was gold first discovered at Sutter's Mill?

5. **UNJUMBLE** these words that have something to do with California. Write your answers on a separate sheet of paper.

   a. **FIAPICC** (HINT: an ocean)

   b. **NMSSIOIS** (HINT: there are 21 of them on the California coast)

   c. **SDEETR** (HINT: a hot, dry place)

   d. **DROOWDE** (HINT: a type of very tall tree)

   e. **PEGARS** (HINT: a fruit)

FOR ANSWERS, SEE PAGE 36.

Glossary

adobe brick: a brick made of dried clay and straw. (p. 9)

brake system: a way of stopping or slowing motion in a car. (p. 26)

cable car: a bus or trolley that runs on tracks and is pulled by a cable. (p. 26)

chaparral: an area that has short evergreen bushes growing close together and with weather that is hot and dry in summer and mild and moist in winter. (p. 21)

computer chip: a tiny, very thin slice of material, such as silicon, that helps to run a computer. (p. 25)

cultures: the customs, beliefs, and ways of living shared by a group of people. (p. 27)

environmental: having to do with natural surroundings and conditions that affect the growth and development of living things. (p. 18)

extinct: no longer living. (p. 21)

fossil: the remains of a prehistoric plant or animal that has become hardened or turned into rock. A fossil might be a skeleton, a shell, a footprint, or the imprint of a leaf. (p. 13)

galaxy: a very large group of stars. (p. 10)

mission: a place where religious and cultural ideas can be taught. (p. 8)

opossum: a small-to-medium-size animal that lives mainly in trees and carries its young in a pouch; often recognized by whitish face, grayish body, long snout, long tail. (p. 20)

Oregon Trail: a historical trail that pioneers used to travel west from

1842 until the development of the railroads; the trail started in the Midwest. (p. 33)

preserved: saved, protected from change. (p. 13)

region: an area of land with no distinct borders. (p. 24)

smog: a fog mixed with smoke; a type of pollution. (p. 18)

tar: a thick, oily dark liquid that's sticky. (p. 13)

Answers to activities on page 34:

1) Nevada and Arizona; 2) Invitations will vary;
3) Answers will vary; 4a) Father Junipero Serra;
4b) mammoth, saber-tooth cat and/or giant sloth;
4c) Mojave Desert; 4d) San Francisco; 4e) 1848;
5a) PACIFIC; 5b) MISSIONS; 5c) DESERT;
5d) REDWOOD; 5e) GRAPES